N.S.A. Parsons studied Art History and English before moving to London to pursue a career in the Metropolitan Police. Throughout this time, he continued to read, to travel and to write. The present volume, *Poems and Notes*, preserves the continuity of these interests to the time of his retirement from the police. He is married and now lives in Hertfordshire.

N.S.A. Parsons

Poems and Notes

AUSTIN MACAULEY PUBLISHERS
LONDON * CAMBRIDGE * NEW YORK * SHARJAH

Copyright © N.S.A. Parsons 2025

The right of N.S.A. Parsons to be identified as author of this work has been asserted by the author in accordance with sections 77 and 78 of the Copyright, Designs and Patents Act 1988.

All rights reserved. No part of this publication may be reproduced, stored in a retrieval system, or transmitted in any form or by any means, electronic, mechanical, photocopying, recording, or otherwise, without the prior permission of the publishers.

Any person who commits any unauthorised act in relation to this publication may be liable to criminal prosecution and civil claims for damages.

A CIP catalogue record for this title is available from the British Library.

ISBN 9781035886364 (Paperback)
ISBN 9781035886371 (ePub e-book)

www.austinmacauley.com

First Published 2025
Austin Macauley Publishers Ltd®
1 Canada Square
Canary Wharf
London
E14 5AA

Table of Contents

Preface	7
1	9
2	11
3	13
4	14
5	15
6	16
7	17
8	18
9 Hastings, from the sea	20
10 Evening, Lucca	21
11 Trastevere, perhaps	22
12 The ghost of a Spitfire, Stevington	23
13 Leaving Blackheath Standard	24
1	25
2	26
3	27
4	28
5	29
6	30
7	31
8	32
9	33
10	34
11	35
12	36
13	37

14	38
15	39
16	40
17	41
18	42
19	43
20	44
21	45
22	46
23	48

Preface

My birth was traumatic; for I was premature, and my mother, with a lack of confidence and ambivalence that was my own inheritance, bled dangerously. I was born by caesarean section; livid, and dying for breath as she was for blood. Her own mother (whose memory was vague) had died when she was a girl, and her father, a veterinary surgeon, in the year that I was born. It was said we were deeply alike, turbulent and intense; but my grandfather was violent, whilst my violence was always contained. What he denied my mother, she gave to me. My father, also a surgeon, was an orphan; though without bereavement, for he never knew his parents. His qualities were equanimity and independence; a foil for my mother's emotionality. His detachment was something I always admired, and my mother said that there was something about him of the Edwardian schoolboy; 'like a child playing alone on the seashore…' A childlikeness that is the most endearing of human qualities, with its carelessness and preoccupation; which makes the life of Newton, for me, the most affecting of all stories.

Of my early life, I remember little, and my school days, I left without regret; my only acquirement, a reputation for buffoonery and underachievement. It was after leaving school that I felt, for the first time, the absence of identity whose fear constrains me still. It was then that I began to read in earnest. And in the summer of that year, I was offered, by chance, the opportunity of a holiday; an art tour to Italy. Of art or Italy, I knew little; but it was to be an encounter which initiated in me, through the revelation of unimagined sensations, a new and larger existence. An experience that lives more vividly for me than any other; so formative of what I love that it calls to me still, like a longing for myself.

University was the beginning of a long and bitter trial, of alienation and emptiness; precipitated by my own behaviour: the beginning of a search for identity through the working out of my unhappiness—a preoccupation that has never left me.

For four years thereafter, I drifted; in a state of indetermination; pathetically unable, or unready, to decide on a course of life. I was galvanised, finally, to join the Metropolitan Police; a career I continue to regard with both gratitude and regret. Later, during a typical period of disillusion, I obtained special leave, and lived for a short time in Rome. Attending a language school, I discovered another life, amongst foreign students; travellers and flotsam like myself. But I was disciplined to explore, and followed an exceptional guidebook through hours of walks and study, alone. In quiet streets, around silent churches, along lonely walls, my individual history dissolved, and I forgot myself in the deep stillness of time. Eighteen months after my return, I married.

Beyond my father and mother, no one has influenced me as the authors I have read. F.L. Lucas, with whom my grandfather corresponded, and the late, modern British school of psychoanalysis; Donald Winnicott, Charles Rycroft and Anthony Storr: who, with their humanity, and feeling for art and ethics, have so shaped and refined me that I will be always indebted to them for their example as men. With these, I wish to include a list of the artists that have meant most to me. For this reason: that I have been created through my contact with them; as touchstones, against whom I have discovered my reality, particularly during the unhappier periods of my life: Nietzsche ('Ecce Homo' and 'The Twilight of the Idols'); Shelley and Byron (in Italy); GM Hopkins; Shakespeare ('Othello', 'Anthony and Cleopatra' and (Burton's) 'Coriolanus'); and on Shakespeare, Harold Bloom. Constable and Turner; Claude and Van Ruisdael; Velasquez and Caravaggio. Beethoven (the violin concerto and piano music); Brahms; and Schubert (the late works). Although I have come to desire, like Nietzsche, what is lighter and more free; so that I now prefer the fierce sadness and serenity of a Pandolfi, and his intimate small oeuvre.

In art, I possessed the rudiments of a talent, which never developed; though the desire for expression persisted. It is to the suggestion of an astrologer (as my young uncertainty craved reassurance) that I owe the small notebook I occasionally keep; whose comments and asides compose a less formal record of my evolution. But it was the illustrative selections of poetry, in the Romantic biographies that I loved, which made me first aspire to order and to concentrate my thoughts as verse. As I began to read, so I began to write. Though never fluent, writing came to me then with a facility that I scarce have found again; and I have come to recognise that I will never be prolific. My ambivalence to composition merely an aspect of the ambivalence that has invested my life.

I must be first compelled by an image or idea. And it is out of this that there grows, as it survives for me, an idea from the image, an image from the idea; born to one another of sustained feeling, that through the other each might find expression in its representation. And the same few representations have obsessed me; like a painter, whose sketchbook is the evolution, through the forms to which he returns, of both his art and self, towards fulfilment and resolution.

And my desire is to leave behind me something enduring, half-secret; a temple in the desert, such as David Roberts drew at Philae or Kom Ombo; whose extant fragments recall the spirit where it lived; which the imagination might inhabit like the wind, finding and longing for meaning. What survives the dissolution and the wreck of time that might redeem and vindicate a life. Notwithstanding, I will live and die with those ghosts that I have loved, knowing that the world has no need of me, or anything of mine.

London, 2012

1

In its intense serenity
Our vast emptiness
Is perfect in the morning sky:
Its inward shine
As luminous and crystalline,
Like impenetrable sympathy;
Where we search our loneliness
In its inspiring silentness:
The consoling cold where hope must ever die.

No pleasure has more awful eyes than wine;
A yearning more rich and deep
For the impossible we still entreat:
Careless helpless unstanchable
Hysterical;
Warm smiling ghastly salt and sweet.
The recognition wastes
The self it tastes
In its staring sleep.
Our dreams in their remembrance decay,
But the gaze of the day
Is void, inscrutable, and grey.

The cloud I regard in my distant fashion;
Beyond all remonstrance,
The unquestionable evening theirs instead,
Abstracted in the golden air.
As mine the ardour and mine the doubt,
The looker-on as their glow goes out,
I gather in insistence and despair:
The recollection in their noiseless passion
I am their desolate romance.
With as pale respect from its purple bed
Desire moves not where the affect is dead.
My completion is the corresponsive dawn,
Chill radiant and blind;
Where my impatience is outworn:
Its unsearchable same sadness find,
Confirmed and chastened to forgo,

In the sufficience I have learnt to know:
As once the church its fervent voices blent
With winter, an ennobled sentiment
As calm profound unconscious as the snow.

2000

2

The far music of fidelity,
That same remembered strain,
Its long returning sad refrain
My inattention sues again,
As if it loved me.
An intercession, like the awakened breeze
With wistful distance stirs
The presiding stillness of the trees,
It always recurs:
The intimate and lonely air of fate,
Which as sure with its movement heaves
The ardour I reciprocate,
Wilful heedless plaintive as the leaves.
Of the hope that I could not forgo,
As a child what it longs for believes,
It as dearly bereaves;
Whose issue's the end we can never know.

My powers suspended as the heavy summer
In discomfortable languor,
I were deaf as its dreaming cloud,
But that I cannot so my heart subdue;
Feverous and proud,
Whilst the dyings that my fantasies pursue
Of others' pleasure

Such elegiac pain inspire
As the pleading of my past,
The infinite and inconsolable desire.
Which mortifies with sudden cold;
As the shadow its substance construes,
Faint against the sky,
Its estranged shape insensibly lose.
The disillusion that I sought to die
Than be longer cajoled.

As from the endlessness it grieves
Distracted, in its prospect of despair,
The child an amusement conceives
That touches its attention unaware.
Unconscious of itself alone
In the sun-spotted shade;
Whose whispers as a smile pervade—
A delight that lifts and flutters with its own.
His present is the wind enthralled,
Whose pleasure cares not where it leads:
The glint and change like emerald;
As music with its tones succeeds,
Eternally discovered and recalled.

2002

3

It rises on an inspiration;
As taking-swift of breath and disbelief
As dolphins, chasing their delight and grief,
Breach into the opalescent wave;
Whose swelling foams with marble pave
Each peak and expiration.
The remembrance that our love pursues;
Like consciousness, to itself appears,
Through the oblivious urge
Of its despairing surge:
As sentience with time coheres,
Whose soundless depth its ecstasies suffuse.

Teasing winds the aspiring cloud
Shear and distress
With eviscerating longing;
Dissolving into air and emptiness
What their loneliness endowed
With substance hope and apprehension:
As meaning in its own contention
Is estranged from belonging.

My teeth in their violence smile:
With brutal hand its mutiny control
Whose weakness still their tender eyes condole,
That pain and purpose cannot reconcile.
Until the impulse returns:
Renewing as the gathering wave
With sobbing crest out of darkness arises;
Whose pitch is the sorrow it recognises;
The remembrance that dolphins crave
As through the opaline shade their ascending pleasure burns.

2006

4

I am the sapphire of the noontide;
The profound and possibility
Beguiling in infinity,
Beyond question will always abide.
Distilled in the silent air;
As sense of a forgotten dream
Conceived in its dissolving stream,
I am imagined of its sweetness and despair.
The stray and wondering affection
That morning resolves
In its milk-white cloud;
To a cream like recollection
Its moving trance evolves,
That stands from its longing, distant, strange and proud.
A poise that feels as stealing-soon
The touch and turning of its afternoon.

Induced of an ungraspable regret
In the fathomless drift of desire,
The apprehension of my shame and pain
Informed by the reach I cannot attain,
I am the substance and abstraction they acquire:
A remembrance still dissolving to forget
As the heart at its freedom contrives;
Whose voiceless agony

In the coils of its contention strives,
Enthralled to its necessity.

As the cloud at its height and culmination,
Whose hours through their change assume
The long first intimation
Of evening, in its slow perpetual bloom:
The unimagined life,
Whose pang is a gaze as far,
Into its wistful deep impels and quickens
The hope that in our aspiration sickens;
Fainting at the utmost that we are.

2008

5

That wound the image of itself discerns
In the sense of its appearing pain:
A smile that my circumstance returns,
Whose abysmal eyes again
Through their dispersing dream,
Aghast into the void of my esteem,
As from a smoke-dark mirror stare.

By shame to that indignity betrayed—
In whose ears the outbreak and the pounding start
Of its chilling smart,
As a flustering conveyed,
Resounds to their crimson and inmost shade
My irrepressible and rising heart.
From the high swell of the departed day
It settles to the shadow-changing deep
And endless restless memory of sleep,
To draw and disturb with profounder sway:
The evocation of my self-disgust;
Whose figuring dreams with envious forms abuse—
As conjuring the phantoms of mistrust—
Things outward with the rancour they accuse.
In that dream of their betrayal to awake:
Deranged by the perception it infects;
As jealousy the motive it suspects,

My fear for their desires I mistake.
Delusion which its circumstance provokes,
To a same vastation palpable and bare
As its secret own despair.

Our fond desire chokes;
The catching snag that undeceives
A sad credulity,
Whose truth itself as suffering conceives:
As a woman's patient empathy
With pain in her sightless reverie,
Through tender thoughtlessness herself perceives.

2010

6

I look out into the past,
As seaward still the Regency serene
Recalls in its gaze, with as rueful cast,
Its prodigal storm-pregnant sky:
A deep-sustained sweet piercing keen,
As our sensibility had been
Created of that passion overpassed.

Though it hang in calm this lee of time,
With ruby eye its wine enticing glows;
The dark-rich fruit soft ripen in repose;
And looming cool in columns and recesses
The quiet church our mystery professes:
A savour so by memory infused
Their contemplation is sublime.

The summer has a yearning which incites
Its reach to a profusion wild:
The plenitude its boughs endues,
With meaning that its redolence imbues
Flush feeling fraught unreconciled;
In lost sensations rapt and blind
The passing of its blue-grey sky invites.

2011

7

Those younger summers in this sky revive,
Whose blue-deepening imagination
Blinks in the brilliance of their intimation;
The delighted climb and cumulation
Of memory its quickening beyond,
As meaning in reflection fond
With that feeling saw when I was most alive.

An earnest of the south, of Italy:
The sun in whom their first becoming glowed
The then dim wilderness of longings strange;
A vision in that light bestowed
Its leaves once more from diffidence persuades.
That intrigue of discovery
To lose itself in vicoli obscure;
Those stones among that its campagna strew,
The fragments of inscription or relief;
With radiance-struck columns range,
As lizard-sudden to allure
With listening heat or patient shades.
Whilst far above in cooler hue
The unheeding autumn gathers in its change.

From which, like a spectre as it hung behind,
I am distracted in the cold set eye
Of my own image,
From that imploring darkness half divined.
The shadows' empty slow encroach
Of time's envious reproach,
In whose void is lost the being I descry.

Into the violet dusk, I turn again,
To a court which breathes in the moss-damp air
With a fountain in its reminiscence lit:
Around the masks of evening thinly flit;
And I am lost in that effusion slow
And soft insisting overflow
Of history my sympathies sustain.

2012

8

As waves from self-possession melt,
With their presumption and identity,
Declining to the sea,
And the light in their confidence dies
To grey-estranged opacity,
We are lost to ourselves:
The braid that its tow unties,
As straining-helpless dissolution felt.

Out of loss the sense collects
Of destiny,
To that sway and sufferance resigned:
Deaf as a three years' child inclined,
With stuffed cheeks sat and sightless eyes alone,
To sadness in a sympathy foreknown;
Whose absence all solicitude neglects
To follow its own pain,
With nature's heedless self-disdain.

By remembrance assumed,
As smoke or breath, in poise, lilt and drift,
I am forgotten on the air:
The waft and lift,
Which plays like vacancy about the door,

And to and back the stubble straw
Stirs with gentle scatter and repair
On the barn floor bare.
Though swifts renew their chase and cry
The summer square and bell tower round,
The glow of evening in the pine trees die,
And breathe magnolia the night's profound;
With her, a dream is passed
That I can find no more.
There is a scent in parting of the sea,
Perpetual-fresh in its eternity;
The longing swell and fall
From which as poignant-brief arose
That moment time must discompose.

From her own pain unreachable to save,
Borne on the bereaving wave
Of her fatality,
She is the grief that cannot choose
But only find itself through what it lose.

2014

9
Hastings, from the sea

It dumbly cries in that identity,
The long offshore and undulating sight:
That near and distant retrospect
With void and fullness heaves in its affect;
The tower which shines in late October light
With sightless still regard upon the sea.
As its stones their warmth outlast:
My drift recalls that lingering way down
The castle cliff, wound by the old town;
Its shadows' fall through damson climb to blue,
Whilst the panes' blaze, backward cast,
My passing answers in their silent view.

Now wink the taverns' lanterns from the quay;
As growing to imagination's ear
The plaining viol and the balladeer
A voiceless pang evoke,
The ribald cheer
To recollection carry, as the wind's throng
The spindrift of the wave, in their rising song:
Who in that reverie and absence yearn
For what is lost to all return.
Whilst in their far regard the fleeting foam,

Which crests and breaks as it awoke
To an infinite brief agony
On the unhearing sea,
With its lapse disperses to darkness home.

10
Evening, Lucca

With patient sympathy, the sun blinks still,
The waiting tender solace of return;
Like smoke the dun cloud passes from the hill
And the gust lulls with gentle unconcern.
New rays enrich with individual life
The leaves air-trailing in the bastion deep,
As inwardly the certainty and strife
Of time their boughs in equal shadow steep.
From crevice dark along the tufted wall,
With drawing blithe and sweet disdaining grace,
The shy swallows break into sudden flight;
Which, flushly though they disappear, enthral
With the free joy that their figurings trace,
That life at last could in itself delight.

2015

11
Trastevere, perhaps

We are estranged by time, whose leaving smiles.
The flowers oblivious its ruins dress;
The long vines darkly hang in emptiness;
And linen brilliant with the warm breeze whiles.
Ensue of ages settle and infill;
To service strange its spolia survive;
As lightly from the low font's shade revive
Its tickling sounds on the smooth stone still.
The cloister's marble walk my ward remains;
Its soundless air with monuments, profound
And garden unregarded of the sky:
Whilst into stranger calm and freedom strains,
From ceaseless generation and redound,
The summer cloud in unheard tumult high.

2017

12
The ghost of a Spitfire, Stevington

Still in its desuetude
The trackless cutting, with the clinging bee
Intent in the flower where they sparsely blow,
Grows close; with throbbing fast to long drone low,
As passing rolls victorious and slow,
And disappears, as lost to memory,
What returns to quietude.

2017

13
Leaving Blackheath Standard

Her teeth protrude in their kindly smile,
Whose asking eyes with her own esteem
Are lost in the hope they cannot redeem,
As the ephemera of summer's stream
Her after-gaze beguile;
Draw, dally and condense,
In their breathing-soft suspense,
With the impalpable and airy sense
Of passing.
As something in her wistfulness takes flight;
To that remove and bosom of the trees,
Where the leaves shimmy but the spoiling breeze
Its sanctity cannot invade or tease,
Like coldness in averted sight.

The late days shine, long, moveless and serene,
With a gentle cool which utters
From beyond all consolation;
Whilst the still first thought down-flutters
Of that evolve to leaving unforeseen.
From windows high the morning new illumes
With ambience the chapel's deep recess.

In amber lucence low
From dim gold the ancient faces glow
Whose life survives the faith that they profess
And light more poignant-strange relumes.

2019

1

....

To flit or trip and dance with light away.

....

As she might search in mine her own desire
So would I too those other eyes require.

2

With pleasure in her far declining I,
And fond regard, now from her prospect turn;
To strain a willing cheek, so shade an eye,
And so desire her not to blind but burn.
How warm we all towards her now; and some,
Still sounding to the skies with easy throat,
Declare their very breath as hers become,
And hers the pathos in each dying note.
But drifts on drifts of flowers as I am dumb;
Half sunk, and lost amid the pungent swell;
As impotent I would that I were numb;
Though never thankless, burning now unwell.
So suffers loss it suffers her again,
And worlds forever onward roll in pain.

1991

3

When unannounced, and from the skies,
Before a golden seam she flies,
This prodigy then sudden dies,
A shooting star.

And glittering, she slashed the deep,
To start me from a hope of sleep;
To light these sullen eyes that weep
For faith in her.

Invested we her liberty,
For such is our necessity:
Propitious were you then to me,
As yet you are.

1991

4

....

When sometimes, for the trespass of her eyes,
  She find forgiving in their touching grace
To let 'em blow in quick new-clement skies:
  'T is even so, as like devolved to earth,
And so surprised by each sweet rebel tear;
  The sorrow of so deep-contending birth
    As patient was in willing to appear.
And is it thus with what we would not own;

....

5

Impatient time, the master of my youth,
How keen you make me study after you,
Who use me with rigour of untruth
That what you have me I entreat to do.
....

1992

6

....

My pleasure still is sickly with the strife
Of fearing for the death that gives it life.

1993

7

The air is parent of its thoughtless play;
And never child was jealous of its care,
Or careless was its jealousies away,
Who never learnt to refuge his despair.
We wander in the rearward of the sun
Distractedly, like rivers in the sand;
And wait, withholding as the tides begun,
The earnest and reproval of her hand.
Though cold with watching we are all on fire:
We love like oceans running with the shore;
Like famished winds with feeding blow the more;
Too eager flames we strangle our desire.
But one greater wish still would our will beguile;
To stand in the inclusion of her smile.

1993

8

The light deceives; where it should make our face,
And with the water should discover us,
It runs away, resolved to colour all;
As eyes with inattention lose themselves,
And idleness neglects the thing it was.
....

1994

9

Desert no longer crowns its own success,
Or wears a shoulder proud to bear the gown,
But conscience checks the person I profess,
As shame had set it high to strike it down:
Like some grand head and fountain of delight
That woos the sun alone with lavish cost,
As honour only shone where he was bright,
Has her vigour glance lustre with him lost.
I am content, so I would nothing lose,
With none at all; though not enough content:
My merits cry, as love has over hope
In his long sleep; though grandeur cannot choose
But grieve with its foundation, and repent
It ever claims for more than it can cope.

1994

10

To taste my purpose needs a salter theme,
Past preservation savours more than youth;
And stronger than recovers to esteem,

....

Our fortune owes us nothing for our grief,
But drinks its sickness into such extremes
As casts the fear that poisons its relief,
With means supply the hunger it redeems.
I am the ice like cold aversion shines,
The smile perceives his moment always past;
A wish to circumstance untimely blind,
I am the pole my circle stills confines.
....

1994

11

....

But such an end I almost lose again,
To think, before I plighted thus to time
The promise so much suffered what it bred,
How expectation made my prospect fine.

....

The same incessance now the summer feels,
Which like a sentiment is in the trees,
Persistent breathing resolution here;
Whose lightest touch as flotsam cannot hold
But almost thoughtless follows to its end.
Reflection the impression of the time
Has stranger made, seem wrong when it was right:
So sentiment most sticks the least secure,
And seems the loath'st to leave what never was.

....

Who sees how like her lovely fingers fall
Suspended in the privacy of thought.

1994

12

The soul of my environs is it she,
The love whose ghost the garden walks alone;
That fancy so constrains to follow free,
Who fears the very threat he feels his own.
Our jealous apprehensions are the same,
As startled in their lightning with excess,
And murder with the touch of their desire;

....

1994

13

Our fretted pleasure whets
This closeness with the sense we faint to meet:
The truth imagination gets,
Where love most loves, is nearest to deceit.
As thoughts are never proof that never feel,
What touch imagines makes its kisses real.

With phantom warmth, our bounds dissolve,
And as we pass in one another seem
The centre of the circle where we dream
Our contraries resolve.

....

The past revives with prospect of success,
And sorrow its same measure in redress.

....

We meet where we least believe
The faith that doubts what kisses most conceive.
And till the rapture, loss is still unreal,

....

1995

14

But my horizon darkens in her brow;
Where utterance was voyage without bound,
My voice has lost its vantage of the prow
Whose same endeavours so exhausted sound.

....

But selflessness plays over every pause,
Forgets to stammer where our thoughts essay,
For confidence creates its own address.

1995

15

As sleep decants the daytime into dreams,
And dreams decant the nighttime into day,

....

Like emperors, that sweeping reins, pull up;
To ride their eyes with prominent command
The host across, their silence cites the form
That would pronounce that this way lies the world.

....

This morning in the greatness of a cloud

....

In likeness even to this brilliant cloud,
Whose rise compounds it in its object's eye,
Embody me the something I compose

....

1995

16

With lace her hands, she trains as fine a nerve
As thorough her the heart its own designs;
Which discipline determines to preserve
The questions our perplexity resigns.

....

As we become the pattern we discern.
A voice pursues the mistress of my ears,
Whose cloister's shadows shiver to resound;
With empathy that makes our times congreet,

....

And as I trace the form my time has found
It masters me to master its conceit.

1995

17

This herald has a pungent nose,
Which swells him with the presence to proclaim;
A perfume apprehensive of the same
Presentiment, September rose.
The need announces her again,
As seasons feel the changes they constrain.

This dream conceives its morning to awake:
My aptness is the circumstance contrives
What the lapse of its remembrance survives,

....

A scent as characters regret,
His person I have met;
Whose mind to lose remembers to forget.

1995

18

Delight in emulation featly steps
Her mistress measure in her own egress.
Whose whispers drew the hair behind her ear;
Enquiring with the face of her demur:

....

She learns the nice conjecture of her foot;
They counterpoise assurances and smiles;
Till fancy, so acquitted to romance,
She starts and colours at her mistress' stop.
Like disenchantment stood in little shoes,
Strangely arraigned in venture of her soul;
This generous disclosure to herself,
And childish affront at compromise,
Forefeels each sad concession to success,
Where every same surrender tries at love.

....

The selfless dedication that she dreams
Is plunging in his deep redemptive heart;
To rush without distinction difference sense,
In broil of bubbles, deaf fervescing light,
A partner danced in ocean's whelming surge.

1996

19

My mother tickles in these pearling tears,
The tense of sensual elegance;
My viscera and comfort where it fears,
She smiles through this extravagance:
The fields that sunshine broadly strays,
As touch our soul discovers where it plays.

Like sympathy, her fingers drain,
To tease my palm relieving her constraint:
The moment that's the mistress I complain;
Whose hardness roles the currance of her plaint.
I am the music so susceptibly
The passion of necessity:
My ruminant and inward working out
A face as time her dream could not misdoubt;
Familiar of infinity.

1996

20

I am proud to feel this wind subdues me;
Sensuous as shame,
Abstracted at the touches that suffuse me;
Wistful of the ardour whence it came.
So distant present stands the evening cloud,
Entranced by the day it has disavowed.

....

....

Now the smile of my own deceiving,
I tarried that shame feel the wind where it grows;
And in this storm and bluster, we strain for leaving.
But pour through these trees and our wait fulfil;
Delightedly complaining still
Exquisite lightnings, that shiver leap and thrill.

1997

21

She is the touch of thought—
This finger barely at my lip,
Whose mind is sense,
And the distraction makes it slip;
Disclose to me the consciousness she taught.
As to myself my eyes decline;
I was the discovery;
The pitch each wave's embrace succeeds,

....

And my heart begins to fail.
I have a look like harrowed winter stares;
As in my teeth it bleakly seethes,
The aching of the hatred that it breathes.
To know himself, though the ghost despairs,
Only the longing can avail.

....

With dignity each step to space,
And suffering, my heart
Controls to efficacy, poise and grace;

....

The roll and sounding of the sea,
In whose swell I hear and swash her song arise:

....

So I possess these feet;
My space and time induce to meet,
Command at last of me what I entreat.

1998

22

I am remembered in the dawn:
A reach distinct in colour its appeal,
Whose implication's feel
Regains like melody;
The struggle into ecstasy,
Rising on each fluttering note,
As certitude in strong convulsions born.

Before my origin of light,
A bitter blind forgiving in my eyes;
The ways I wandered with return on me
As the orient of memory,
And petulance looks childishly contrite.
I was leaving when I recognised
This sadness in the fate that I despised,
That hope must watch till its illusion dies.

As I deeply breathe
The birds inspired summon in the air;
Whose single rhapsody,
Like the lapse of water rising through itself,
Sways to a thoughtless harmony
In their wayward sympathy,
And the exaltation that they dare,
My spirit in the morning I bequeath.

A frost had hardened in my face
The suspense of my frigid atmosphere:
The thrall of soundless space,

....

And staggered grief in mounting reparates,
As some great gull the feeling vindicates
Of life, over the grey-green ocean clear.

A child in my prophetic trance,
I turned away to what I deeply knew;
As possibilities with my impatience grew,
And the freezing anguish they excite:
Desire is a destiny,
Whose trial is its chastity;
The strength to bear the end our eyes advance.

I rouse, as filling in me it appears;
The sense persuades my look behind.
Which recollection brings it on;
As the streams that in the new sun glisten
To the woods and ageless hills that listen:
An earnest in this moment find,
Whose high descant and dance of pain remind
Deserves what our life endears.

1998

23

Her starts at chance incredulous betray
The phantoms of possibility:
In whose look the instance cannot live,
Though all her willing charm delay.
To the despair of vanity;
Whose wry eyes approve the smile it cannot see;
Elusive and deceiving as the air—
The jest apparent, but the joker nowhere.
My hope is jaded, sick and pale,
And wants a reverence in its self-regard;
As virtue, high unsparing hard;
Its reproach and expectation.
For like an epicure desire is stale
Of envy and contempt, and its will perverse
As lust, love's dark obverse.

Something is lost to the day,
That slips with the sleight of its stream;
Through the hours of the shade led away
With the lilt of its flies, in a moment's gleam.
The wreck of everything foregone:
Ready and late and slow and soon
It follows as flotsam the piper his tune;
With a reflection like the still sun
Of times when there wanted none.

The thought swoons of the passing year:
The moving pause allowed
Of its strange familiar cloud;

....

As autumn answers, shining, cold and clear,
The steps its very silence makes aware
Of their question of mortality:
Like the blind who know the way they walk,
With fatal patience unperturbed;
The whisper waiting of divinity,
Whilst the wide demean of loss stands undisturbed.
What are we, whither do we go:

Our chorus rises in its own reply;
Of its despair imploring so
The impossible and empty sky.
In their condolence our voices compete,
Rich peerless steady sonorous replete;
The infinite suspense hold tremulous;
Beyond all mortal strife,
A lament so beautiful of life
I am terrified to die.

There now pervades the evening clime,
And kindles in its soulful face,
What circumstance detains to time.
Consumed in an unearthly hush,
Rapt bewildered faint and flush;
Subsumed into sublimity.
In its ethereal trance
Of sadness serenely deposed;
What loss can no farther beguile.
With desolation in my burning glance
I wait against oblivion;
In the imagination of myself composed.
And yawning my impatience, I find her humour so;
As the possession that could let her go:
An urge respect cannot suppress, to smile;
For really nothing laughs but the abyss.

1998

The distraction that is not preoccupation but hurt and intransigence.

As neurotic anxiety is resolved in the same character to an ideal of elegance and grace (Van Dyck).

The guilt that steps, as it were, beneath admonishment.

The more we experience of privation, the more obdurate do our feelings become.

Something equivocal; like a spirit in the wind.

How much sympathy is only emulation?

Not acting, but finding a part in which to exist at all.

Play a part to feel it in ourselves.

To touch a thing, allude to it, as it were, far off, because it touches one too nearly.

Identity is a physical experience.

Emulation is an affinity and feeling after ourselves.

Attraction that impels a rich perfume.

Silence is more recognition than any acknowledgment.

Generation grows throughout remembrance.

Feelings are modified through time, but their history and sequence are preserved.

In great art, symbolisation is the counterpart of sense experience; as Palmer's 'Brilliant Cloud', which could be conceived only through the assimilation of many such brilliant clouds, is at once immediate and eternal.

Form is the perfection of feeling, as feeling is of form; and by their integration through art is achieved the sense of necessity, where subjective and objective are one.

An abstract and feminine perfection; which does not partake of the moment, but composes it.

The complex of feeling, unfathomable in itself, that is summed up and expressed in a single action or reaction.

There is something impersonal behind the working out of feeling; a logic that subtracts interaction, and the timing of the most intimate and personal gesture.

Unless we live for something beyond ourselves, our lives can confirm nothing.

The quiet and circumspection of a secret love around the thing it loves.

To affect an accent, or appearance, or behaviour, infers an unassimilated trauma and unhappiness.

The feeling of fadedness most coincides with the feeling of freedom and self-determination. When I have felt powerless to effect anything, I have suffered most in contingency.

Depression is a conspiracy of many causes.

Illusion is always more potent with us until we meet reality.

We are most serious in our pleasures.

We meet what we fear in those ways (where) we had hoped to avoid it; as we meet what we hope for in those ways (where) we do not expect it.

In the anxiety and despair of prolonged frustration and disappointment, there is engendered an exquisite feeling for the flow and ceaselessness of things: for the wind in the trees; for pathos in music; and for the poignancy of passing time.

My life seemed no longer the subject of my own volition, but I was evermore confirmed in the awful feeling of necessity; which deepened my experience of myself in a way that I was afraid to follow, could I have willed it otherwise.

The sincerest gifts are made with a reticence that looks more like indifference.

The feeling of exquisite sadness that we are alive, and must relinquish our brief moment to eternity, as to the sun rising.

Sentiment is for that dawn of new experience to which we can never return.

The apparent lack of interest in what one says, which is the feeling that one is oneself uninteresting.

Malice disappears when one finds the courage for one's own life.

It is not regret, but an engendered vague emptiness and longing.

Pathos is insipid, unless it is played with strenuousness and vigour.

There is more suffering in contingency than in all the rigour of necessity.

Our pasts and futures grow and change, mature and die; and there is a harvest time for both; for the fiction of our lives must find its own artistic truth.

A feeling like the monumental calm of ruins; which has the poignance of other, nobler ways of life, that have passed into silence.

The great virtues are both self-affirming, and life affirming.

Virtue is preserved by beauty; character degraded by ugliness.

Our feelings remain, only the perception of their subject changes. Their tide must achieve a fullness within us before their special intensity begins to recede forever. When this change is imminent, they are at their most puissant and persuasive, and the feeling that one can never finally overcome them is the immediate prelude to their decline. One then experiences one's feelings in their entirety, and their conclusion is this sum of their subject's symbolic power.

As consciousness is the perfection of thought, unconsciousness is the perfection of action.

Fadedness is something we achieve; perhaps something we are fated to achieve.

What happens to oneself is as much a part of oneself as what one causes to happen.

The music (as Beethoven) where there is felt a deeper sense of necessity; that evolves, and that discovers itself.

Grace is the mind made articulate through the body.

She kept clearing her throat as she spoke, giving her intended intimacy an awkward formality.

Our mutual distance as we walked together was always according to the unspoken harmony between us; which seemed to draw us together or apart.

There is a cool and inviolable calm in the blue of the summer sky, like perfect abstraction; and I know of only one artist, Richard Parkes Bonnington, to have painted it. It is an attitude to the sky as consolation.

Only with prolonged meditation on a thing can one involve its more profound associations.

She moves in her grace without thought; except where her pain obtrudes, in the antagonism of something she cannot reconcile (Velasquez's 'Portrait of a Woman').

I am told I laugh at inappropriate moments; but it depends on precisely where one sees the joke.

A loud laughter, deaf to pain and pathos.

Profound impressions are created unconsciously, and can never be contrived.

We are real to one another in so far as we touch reality, and in so far as we possess it.

As our conversation is involved on so many levels, we cannot know what we mean to say.

We are all also somewhere else, whence we receive strange and fearful intimations.

I would not exclude, from any conception of my own necessity, the feeling for those realms of the beyond; where the imagination of possibility, or the possibility of imagination, is the glow at the horizon, where I can never see whether I rise or set.

There is a fitness in behaviour, which is relatively absolute.

Wherever else we have vanquished God, He is still the terror in ourselves.

There is no argument against God (for myself) that the voices of Thomas Tallis could not confute; which implore His *absence*.

In a heightened state of awareness, the metaphorical value of circumstances and behaviour becomes more obvious; particularly in a heightened state of relatedness.

Lying down is worst for suffering.

My greatest pleasure would be for her to feel that with me she could be herself, as with no one else.

A dialectic that obtains between persons; who, as they continue as aspects of each other's self-experience, must needs have found a deeper affinity.

How certain are those subliminal impressions which compose our instinctive feelings, when those feelings cannot be separated from our construction of them; the confusion of our hopes and fears.

Our continuity for one another is our only standard of certainty; that our recurrence for one another continues to have meaning and significance.

We will meet each other again; because our feelings were not resolved. Our circumstance must needs contrive to bring us to that resolution.

The collusion between people, where one causes oneself to be seen, though oneself was unaware.

The end is the last act after which the significance for both is meaningfully diminished.

At one's weakest and unhappiest, when one most needs judgement, one wants it most.

The consciousness of them lies on me like a sense of suffocation.

On the portrait of an unknown man by Velasquez. Depth resolved in surface; timelessness in the instant; objectiveness in the subject; the type in the individual; the palpable in the spiritual and ethereal; the personality in its contradictions; stillness in flux and change; reality out of its shadows and illusions; endurance in evanescence; and everything permanent, real and substantial, out of transitoriness.

Not just to listen, but to see the pianist touch the keys into music.

Some moments are perfect, and have that quality of sublimity in which we stand in an eternal relation to ourselves.

I enacted passion with her, in simulation of the desire I felt, but not for her; and which she both mistook, and understood.

When a man tripped on a paving stone, and a crew of builders roared with laughter, what I found amusing was *their* reaction.

How and why must ultimately become the same question.

On a portrait by Goya in the Courtauld. The subject possesses time; as it contradicts the flow and reading of the painting by moving against the timeless stillness of those relations around it. But it is the stillness of these relations that has the feeling of impermanence, as the unsettling motion of the subject, in its relation to these, makes it only more real, more there. The artist does not try to fix the subject by excluding time, which alone can animate the subject, and make it live; but to suggest it as within time, like an impediment in the stream, which comes into being as it defies, for a moment, time's oblivion.

My happiness enables me to feel and understand sadness; and the desire beneath all success, like an undersong, which is a longing for oblivion.

That quality in wine, which enlarges emptiness and desire the more one drinks.

The circumstances of that evening were traceable to the morning, when an unconscious influence was beginning to be felt; which, like the moon in the day, was present, though unseen. And as I grew in feeling and consciousness, my circumstance became apparent: the circumstance becoming the consciousness and actuality of my unconscious process.

It is in pain that our character is formed, or destroyed: to possess itself and what it loves; or to lose itself and what it loves, forever.

The need to deserve happiness: which is the satisfaction in myself that I have overcome my weakness; which is the tenuousness of all possession, both of oneself and of the other.

She could never have foreseen that I would see it, nor could I infer that it was left for me to find, but that the fact itself was eloquent.

The deepest communion is with oneself, even in the act of love. One only gazes on, only imagines, oneself; for in less than love, one sees only the other.

A sadness so thoroughly infused, it generates a radiance without taint of melancholy.

Hamlet finally has the courage to die to this life when he overcomes that dread of the thought of something after death. That hereafter becomes the story of himself, which he entrusts to Horatio. One must have recovered hope in this life to die to this life; which, in Hamlet's case, is the retrospective hope of consolation; that in his story, there is finally purpose and significance enough to justify his suffering. This significance he finds in the end, both in itself and as end.

It seemed to me that those who cried 'Freedom, liberty, enfranchisement', after the murder of Caesar, were like so many schoolboys escaped from the sweet shop; who do not want what they have stolen, but the thrill of stealing it, and who are as likely to throw the same sweets at one another, or stamp on them, as actually enjoy them.

That skilful tact, which, without offence, made me aware of myself.

She laughed, as she was superior to laughter: as if one could be superior to laughter.

If our political correctness had been around in Chaucer's time, one of his pilgrims would have made a tale about it, and everyone would have laughed.

What we begin to take for granted begins to think of leaving us.

The only way to play Beethoven is to try to outdo him in passion and pathos (which implies neither speed nor lack of control).

There are only necessities: what we call contingency is that perspective on the necessity we have not achieved. A new sense of necessity is achieved over ourselves.

Where we search for meaning, that meaning is often the very absence and uncomfort.

I have seen women cry for what they cannot feel.

I hope that in the first person, I may become more personal and impersonal.

I have a strange fixation that I must anticipate something for it not to be the case in fact.

The acuity that we learn of Shakespeare, whose characters continually ignore, or misconstrue, what is said to them; or ask, or answer, as if they addressed only themselves.

What if there were no fadedness between us, and our fidelity to one another were merely faith. How much nobler to overcome in ourselves the need for fadedness; and perhaps, out of this faith, there comes fadedness in fact.

I was reminded, at court, of the lesson, that one can make any number of excuses for oneself, but one is judged only on the performance, and only the performance is remembered.

The portrait of Nicholas Lanier, by Van Dyck, is so engaging because the subject possesses self-consciousness; appearing to retreat from scrutiny, making us wonder at ourselves.

As one moves on the water, through his lucent atmospheres, one feels one's substance and distinctness but momentary; for where one has come from every moment is dissolving in infinity. The farther one sees, the more one's bounds seem endless; and as one gazes into his distance, water, earth and sky are lost in one element (Van Goyen).

Possibilities are our greatest seduction: one must develop an ear for the more difficult music of one's true life—'the life one does not live'.

There is something in the reality of her face that is beyond love and is touching the other; something that is beyond oneself, and dear as one's own loneliness and mortality. Perhaps only in the other, does one touch that loneliness and mortality.

Perhaps modern medicine encourages illness in a way unknown before, with the security one now has in falling ill.

I take her sudden sleeps as a tender sadness for herself; where rising hope confronts a rising despair of hope, and of herself.

My feelings and affects, whilst they evolve, tend to recur; from which I infer a generative centre, or self; which I can evade but cannot escape, because they always refer me to it. Whilst this centre, or self, may not be susceptible of proof, the way I experience is my greatest certainty. For I am certain of myself as I experience myself in feeling; and feeling must have a self that feels, or it is meaningless. For how can pain, which is mental suffering, and entirely dependent on the way one feels, exist at all, except in relation to myself—the complex of everything I feel. If those feelings did not tend to that constructive relationship, the self, and suffering not recur in the particular ways that it does, it would be arbitrary, and irrelevant; and needless to feel at all. No one can choose not to feel, except to believe that pain is suffered by other than oneself. Reiterated experience constructs a sense of self, as the thing to which happenings occur; and as our experience creates ourselves, so it belongs to ourselves, for we are inseparable from it, and incomprehensible without it.

I have needed to overcome the intensity and unhappiness of my feelings; which I relate to a sense of powerlessness and abjection; and learn to wait, in order that my experience can actualise. It is the waiting, for me, which has been unbearable; and the course of my life, a lesson in patience and self-control.

Eustacia's passion would have been exorbitant had she lived even in Paris; and the wastes of Egdon are its appropriate reality, an eternal emptiness.

Our dearest wish, which continues irrespective of hope, is the pole star of our life; and is begotten in us as the most precious thing that we have lost.

I wonder if the fullness of grief is not its satisfaction too.

There are times in one's life that can never be redeemed; and though one might try to reconcile them, that without them, one could not have come to that understanding of oneself that one now has, they remain, like a void or emptiness, beyond everything one can ever enjoy, a pain in one's heart that can never be removed.

A mother's mind that imagines for another.

God is remoter than I ever imagined.

There was something wonderful and poignant in the steadiness of his hand, and the still clarity of his signature.

The inconsolable crying in all fantasy and dependency—though its voice is suppressed—that is the crying after one's own self.

Our pride is forgiven us—but never our want of humility.

Napoleon's Russian campaign: the suffering, the disasters, the atrocities, the heroism, the loss of life… And yet, there is something in the idea, the mythology, of Napoleon, which seems to justify it all.

I have lived with the fear of death for what I've loved as if I had carried that death in my experience itself. To have found that death in myself, I have died as it were to save the thing I love, as I now believe that it does not have to die.

When I read Johnson, in his imagined massive, pompous tones, it makes my toes curl with pleasure.

Is conscience absolute, or only relative to ourselves? Conscience is born of love, and where no love is, there is the shadow or privation of conscience; which searches for conscience as conscience searches for love.

As old people are struck with sleep; as they were seized in the dark wave of something bearing towards oblivion.

The shadow of idealism is despair.

It is not desire that is infinite, only illusion.

When I considered why I had made no impression there, it was that my interest had withdrawn: it was as ghostly to me as I was ghostly.

To attain the present, one touches something eternal and beyond time.

As during periods of extreme stress or unhappiness, one's opinions tend to polarise.

There is something mocking my serious sadness, as a self-absorption or narcissism; as that sadness was my alienation itself.

The significance of a relationship is what it enables and brings out in oneself; in respect of the other, the person one becomes.

What I really want is not my fantasy.

What is the purpose of our lives: we seem to lose it even as we ask the question.

It is strange that Keats, who so doubted his own identity, should be so loved for his identity; which, we feel, was his passionate identification with what he loved.

Empathy is not merely the capacity for identification with the other, but has also a coldness and objectivity, which disdains all sentimentality; as Velasquez finds in his final portraits of Phillip IV.

Memory is an abstraction, and stands at one remove; and in our intensest pleasure and intensest pain, we are closest to oblivion. The pain or pleasure that we remember has a poignance which recollects itself at a distance, and flows into itself, as into an absence, where oneself was somewhere else. Whilst in our intensest moments, we are identified with our pleasure or pain, in memory, we are identified with ourselves at a distance, at one remove.

There is a benign and a malign irony to our lives, which we pursue according to our conscience.

The pleasure we find when what we have dimly felt is represented to us as meaningful, and beautiful.

We flirt with *im*possibilities.

Conscience, in opposing itself to our persisted actions, alters over time our perception of what we do, to conform with itself; so that, rather than effecting change, as by an act of will, the actions that we could not give up, we come to give over, as things estranged from us.

I wonder if there is an oblivion of memory, where what is redundant is finally forgotten; not just to consciousness, but as if it never existed.

We move with such cognisance of space and time, that we find meaning in coincidence; as we knew where to find it.

Often there is as much significance in what does not happen to a person.

It seemed that within myself was the indistinct comprehension of everything I would become, and, even at the dawn of my becoming, the deepest understanding of what I was. So that it was necessary only that that self should find itself; and the bringing into consciousness of that self was my purpose and fulfilment.

The execution is concise as the feeling is concentrated.

I caught her unexpectedly, without her knowing, in an attitude I had not seen before, but which was strange and beautiful to me: as if she had wanted me to know something deeper about herself; as if she had wanted me to see it. She had stooped and taken the child's hand, as she were the child; with her eyes glazed, as she saw only herself.

With illusion, we also overcome the morbidity and jealousy of our longing and unhappiness; as we no longer desire what will not give itself.

The loss is real when it has no illusions left.

The things that I love about her I will not tell her, in case she become self-conscious.

Something in her attitude, without thought; of depth, soulfulness, and experience; more eloquent of who she was than she could ever speak.

We must finally resign ourselves to that higher consciousness, whose discernment alone knows what we really want. And it occurs to me that to have attained to this resignation is the justification for everything that I have undergone, and possibly, my only means to have attained it.

I had a dream last night in which I was shown by my father how to sacrifice a calf. And the calf had great soft eyes, that made an appeal to me stronger than any human eyes; and the feelings of this dream resolved themselves, thus: that so long as one cannot sacrifice her, and walk away from her, one must continue to lose her; but when one can sacrifice her, and walk away from her, then one possesses her forever.

It is the very things that one tries to evade that become ineluctable and inescapable.

I have found myself responding to things in a more perfunctory way, without appetite; and continuing to do what I no longer feel: as if there were a lag in time, between the overcoming of a habitual stimulus, and one's physical disengagement from it.

Childishness is wilful, petulant, and self-conscious, to the same degree as childlikeness is free, delightful, and unconscious of itself.

I remember in English once, the teacher trying to be funny on Macbeth, and my friend turning to me and writing, 'I 'gin to be a weary of the sun'.

There is a time beyond despair, where we meet what we thought we would never find. But one has first to accept despair to get beyond it; for despair is the without which not of all recurrence.

When I have addressed to her something I have truly meant, I have spoken to her without seeing, and been aware only of my own words, as they had spoken themselves.

I had a dream—that I sat on the edge of an abyss, where there was a little boy, and I said to him, "Our fears are our desires, and that very fear of the abyss is drawing me towards it."

As originally, she came back from despair, from the abyss; so it is only from the same despair that she can come again.

At the end of illusion is the end of despair.

When [ ] had an inexplicable nosebleed during dinner, the thought occurred to me, flippantly, 'the life they cannot find', with the refrain from Dracula, 'the blood is the life'. And the strange concatenation of circumstances, or ideas, that could have led to it, which remain unfathomable; except this always holds, that the fact speaks for itself.

Despair haunts all illusion as an undersong; and where I had thought to have met despair, at the end of illusion, I find no such thing; for illusion is the secret of despair.

With the despair, it is the senselessness that I have sought to find; to restage and to relive. And I have sought this senselessness, not in order to make sense of it, but to experience it within my capacity to comprehend it as such.

The circle is not broken whilst we are still waiting for return.

A hidden church—the last of incense hanging in the air—black-red wine—and candlelight—to peruse some forgotten master painting by Caravaggio.

A feminine faintness and fatality; as women in pain, who accidentally cut themselves, watch themselves bleed, with something like curiosity and satisfaction, that what they feel they can see.

Often, in falling in love, we are driven by a compulsion to suffer, as if we needed to restage our primal dramas of abandonment and despair. Our desire to escape the pain of these dramas is our flight to safety in relations; but this very need for control is most subject to the irony of falling in love.

What recurs, when one no longer waits, comes back to one freely, as it loves; and recurs forever.

It appeared to me that in the period leading up to that day, the day on which everything would determine, I had suffered proleptically all the pain of separation; and that the day had been long prepared for and decided. My suffering was the process of our separation, which, until that day, was still unconscious to me.

I had a dream, that she came to me, and said to me that her greatest wish was to change her sex; which, with the feeling one has in dreams, I understood as a confidence that she could not bear to be a woman. And later, as it flowed from the former dream, I dreamt that we sought the murderers of a child; which, with the same feeling for her, I understood was herself.

What would it mean to lose her, if one was so identified with her as to be inseparable from her. One could only contemplate the total loss of oneself. For to be able to lose her, one must have found one's self, one's identity, without her; the sense of self that can conceive of itself independently, however it identifies with what it loves.

One has to achieve identity before one can lose oneself without the fear of annihilation. And it is as one acquits oneself to, and is able to tolerate, being brought to nothing, that one finds identity; for identity is founded on nothing. And nothing is felt as real, nor as possessed, nor as valuable, until it has been lost, and despaired of. Identity is what survives nothing. 'Be that thou knowest thou art, and then thou art/As great as that thou fear'st'. This is the great exhortation to nothing; the nothing which is our greatest fear; and the hardest thing is to let go of what we are not for that fear of nothing.

Repressed behaviour which is unconscious; and freedom from repression of affect; which is unconscious as it is unself-conscious.

In all self-gratification and indulgence, there is an obtrusive and petulant 'I'; which is as ugly as it is insistent.

In the insane, we often see an affected unself-consciousness, which is acute self-consciousness; and which appears as an endeavour at the unself-consciousness of children. In fact, it is nearer to the unself-consciousness we achieve when we become ourselves, and are oblivious to our environment and its impingements, as we cease to care for them.

I couldn't see how her circumstances could be more than adventitious, or merely contingent; before I saw, in his dark obsession with her, the reflection of her own perverse desire for admiration, and the collusion she would never admit for her own vanity.

The evolution of dreams, as of all symbolic relations, as they continue to evolve, remain obscure to us; as we are to ourselves. Except that at significant moments, they achieve a perfection of expression which is perfect meaning.

We live in the experience of becoming; which confers on persons and places all that we remember of meaning and value.

There is an accumulation and swell of pain, which seems to rise from memory and desire, towards expression, and self-consciousness; but whose intention we continue to subvert, because we cannot bear its intensity.

As in a dream, there is the text, and the object of the text, which we identify as ourselves, and which it provokes into feeling and emotion; so in our waking life, there is our circumstance and ourselves.

The secret of memory is its infusion with feeling; so that to memorise a thing we must first imagine it.

In pain, there is a crying after meaning and understanding; and our suffering is only unbearable where, like a child, we cannot find it.

The feelings that our circumstances make actual are not just the consequences of those circumstances but actually their cause. The self-hatred I feel at my excess is the very motive for that excess.

There is a philosophy in the music that I love that has the rhythm of a dance; whose grace and certainty is shot through with skittering lightning; and which resolves me and reconciles me to myself more than reason can.

I find in Vivaldi, a wonderful quality of impersonality; that is in the sights and smells, the light and atmosphere, of what he loves: where the self-lives most freely in the life outside it.

When things lose their aim, as the Parthian darts at Anthony, our actions are informed by a bad conscience, and that aim taken out of spite or envy.

What incurs injury is in itself damaged, sick or injured.

I could never love again the person she was.

Our greatest terror is arbitrariness.

The voice rises in proportion to what is suppressed.

I had a dream, that I was attacked from the deep by a great white shark: and as it lunged at me, in my horror and revulsion, with a spear gun, I shot it through the head. And as I saw it convulse, with its rolling eyes thrown back at me, as they sought me in their pain, I recognised a horror of mortality, of life and death, that almost choked me. And as it profusely bled, it stayed for me in the foam, that I might remove the barb embedded in its head: which, as I did, and as it slipped away, I could have held it for pity.

There is the pleasure of first discovery, which is an awakening into a life richer in possibility. There is the pleasure of closeness and growing intimacy with what one learns to love.

And there is the pleasure, more intense, of that encounter, with the thing we have discovered and have learnt to love, which startles and suffuses us with forgotten feelings, and unites us with our deeper life again.

My most emotive memories, of the dawn of new experience, in their recollection, are suffused with something of Turner's Italian light.

The taste of ourselves, as opposed to our illusions, is bitterer, but savours more.

In our dream of oneness, the act of love has a death in it, which is the destroyer of illusions. Which we survive as we are real for one another.

The effort of thinking on our most difficult problems, is the effort required to think outside one's habitual mode of thought.

It is not the emptiness that makes the longing, but the longing the emptiness; like a vastation, in which the condition of longing is such that it can never find satisfaction.

The permanent change wrought by that torment, as my mind had been actually recast.

The doppelganger is the projection of our estranged selves.

I have a mind that has learnt less to remember than to forget.

Idealism, unhappiness, and intemperance, appear to me now in a special relation.

My mother's inability to detach herself from her abusive relationship with her brother, suggests to me that he expresses an anger and self-destructiveness that is her own.

There appeared to me a dialectic between myself and my experience, that gave me what I asked, but with a knowingness that posed a more searching question.

Turner's Italian light is the present beheld as memory.

That quality of isolation as the condition of human life, which Caravaggio finds in all his figures, who forever evade each other's eyes.

The fear of loss is a continual feeling of undeserving.

Our construction of the past depends very much on how we regard ourselves in the present.

The glint off the waves, that flashed upon me as sensations of forgotten pleasure, suffusing me with what appeared like ineffable pain.

It is not what I have lost of childhood that fascinates me, but what I retain.

Maturity and ripeness steals though us as colour into fruit.

With readiness, choice and necessity become the same.

Trying to follow her vague self-consciousness, it occurred to me she must be drunk.

Mental conflict is subsequent to happenings, until one is strong enough to overcome a thing in imagination, where containing conflict pre-empts happening.

In the shipwreck of our lives, with its abandonment of so much that we want to believe in, there is really very little worth holding onto; except, perhaps, the phrase, of music, of poetry, or of paint, that alone survives in our heart of hearts.

The relationship between our circumstance and ourselves is particularly seen where our irritation and frustration in events makes conscious and manifest the unhappiness that before we but dimly felt.

The behaviour we dismiss in others as exceptional on their new acquaintance, invariably, we come to see is habitual to them, and expressive of what they are.

Brahms' music, and the violin concerto particularly, recalls to me the time when I first heard him; when, despite the emptiness of my experience, my life had a quality of rich agony, where I felt my own abysmal possibilities as I never have again. And to recall those feelings makes me bitter and grateful to have refound a part of myself.

The effect of unhappiness cannot always be traced to a cause, either imaginary or real, but is as often simply the distress of change, whose strain and contortion, like lava, adapting to its own pressure, must break its former crust; and cool, only to be breached again.

Her identification with fairies is with that secret and twilight life which she inhabits on the fringes of reality; not her own but others'. For she has learnt to live with the unpresuming modesty of everything overlooked, but that appears to a child's curiosity, like hedgerow flowers, or ladybirds, or butterflies; what is like herself, and exists, perhaps, only in her own imagination.

What sort of death wound must he (Keats) have suffered, what irrecoverable loss, that so much passion, violence, and life, should, notwithstanding, want to die.

I look back with envy, almost, on that pain, whose openness and susceptibility took such a deep impression, of art and its reconciliations, that my feeling for it now is as a recollection of my own passion.

Those impressions we receive in the periods of our greatest pain are more profound and formative; and all our subsequent response is a feeling after and recollection of what we once have felt.

A sexless nature, that lacks the self-consciousness that women have even when unobserved.

Touches that before I would not have recognised, are now meaningful, as being meaningful to her.

I imagine that out of the ability to be alone (which was the gift of her attention), the desire to be alone, and to preserve a part of myself inviolate, beyond the appropriation of her moods, began my intolerance of all appropriations; and the drift, ever since, of my attention to myself. For, as long as I can remember, my ability to listen has been compromised by a lack of concentration, to recall instructions, or to master detail, which has always shamed me. The preoccupation of my privacy has been the place where I have existed without interruption, and where I have preserved my continuity for myself.

As we see ourselves, so others see us.

She hiccupped at the perceived objection in my tone.

I no longer take my dreams so seriously; for they are rarely an elucidation of an objective reality, but rather distended states of subjective emotion; which exaggerate my jealousy, hatred, or hostility, in such a way that I infer an objective reality as against their extremities, lacking the context and perspective of my waking life.

She has an endearing quality of treating me often as merely part of her subjective world; playing with my hair with that regardlessness as I was some imaginary large creature, which children befriend where adults take fright.

There is a self-portrait of Velasquez in the Capitoline museum. Hid in an obscure corner, and stated as of doubtful attribution, it held me for hours, and seemed to me to be by far the finest piece in the collection. By the quality of the painting alone, it was clear that it could be by no one else.

Her toes engrossed in comfort; as seaweed in the ocean's stream curls and uncurls.

Wondering how the quality of childlikeness survives in individuals, it occurred to me that in refusing to be assimilated, it continues for the reason that it first became detached; as a refuge, whose space and privacy preserves a place where one can continue to exist, free and to none appropriated.

On the death of Anthony, Cleopatra begins her grand revision: where she confronts at last her fear of commitment, both to him, and to her own destiny.

Not superficial confidence, without doubts; but self-possession, with a deeper certainty, feeling its insufficiency; as a deep wound which refuses to close.

From the oppression of weariness and constraint, the waves of my sentient life, unconscious to me, but exaggerated by their long suppression, were caught by a melody; whose rhythm, as a ship to the sea, accorded to them with such sympathy that their movement became conscious; with a thrill that shook me with my own emotion, as I had discovered that life again.

The instinct for decision which thinking only serves to confirm.

The utmost of its intensity was in my struggle to keep it down, whose involuntary utterance was its only relief.

She left her fingers in my hair, with a gentle distraction, like the sea's wash and drain around the brown-wet fastness of a rock.

Art consumes the fire of its creation, as the expression of ourselves consumes our life, in becoming what we are.

A problem which has preoccupied me, with more wondering than progress, is where I end and the objective world begins; what belongs to me, and what I must attribute to a causation not my own; how far I determine, and how far am I determined. It irritates and distracts me, the approach of another person when I am walking alone. On such an occasion, when their presence began to impinge on me, my heel struck sharply a small stone, at precisely the angle to make a 'crack'; surprising myself and my passer-by with an awkward consciousness of one another. The act was unconscious, nor could I consciously repeat it; and it occurred to me that I had involved what was external to me (the position of the stone in place and time) to contrive the circumstance (the 'crack' that had surprised us both with consciousness of one another), which had not only betrayed me to my passer-by, but made me conscious of myself, of my irritation.

I love untold stories. We comprehend, are willing to comprehend, almost nothing of *why* things happen. The man stabbed to death at a bus stop. The woman in crossing struck down in the road. There is an unexpressed life to which our insight is largely blind; which is manifest as much in what happens to us as what we cause to happen. Are we not then more profoundly connected with the world in which we move, and do we not have greater cognisance of ourselves, in space and time, than we are aware of, or understand.

I do not love humankind, but hold the individual to be the final measure of the value of existence.

The accumulated resentments and disappointments that, were I to speak them to my friend, would estrange him from me forever; which withholding, will forever estrange me from him.

There is no piece of music which better illustrates, for me, the necessary coherence of strong feeling with rigorous form in all high art than 'Spem in Alium': a work whose sublimity of emotion is entirely dependent on the observation of its architectural formality, and which degenerates into meaningless chaos where there is heard merely its outpouring of feeling. Its feeling becomes meaningful, becomes moving, only where it is articulate, coherent and distinct; as conducted, for me, by Sir David Willcocks.

In the half-light, I imagined her as one of Caravaggio's angels; those pale and supple figures, in their strange empathy, reaching out of darkness.

My prosody has been merely a listening to myself, in the dark.

That jealous mind which must recognise its own desires as those it fears in others.

One must always make an exception for individuals.

As (bodily) wind expresses an unspoken objection.

That awakening before the dawn, when we are visited, at our bitterest and most disconsolate, by the ghosts of the buried day.

It is inevitable to me that the same mind should feel at once the fitness and propriety of where it is, of what it has, and the awful longing, in rebellion, to be somewhere else.

Her thought-tickled feet, as sensing my delight.

It is the end of anxiety to wear out its causes to indifference.

A suspense of distance, beyond all but the imagined sound (Claude).

Despite my hatred, the object of my enmity is as much a provocation to my agon with myself.

We can never find again the places we have loved, for that time has been transfigured, in its own imagination; and exists no longer, but as experience, in time.

An itch, the irritation and reminder of a suppressed restlessness, dissatisfaction and desire.

I can hardly imagine a greater pleasure than to watch Velasquez, in his maturity, in the act of painting: not just imagining what he saw, but creating in paint the sensations, the feel, and empathy, of seeing. As painting and apprehension were the same, to represent the immediacy of those sensations, and in its substance catch, as they compose and dissipate, the moods of his mind. As meaning concentrated where he most intensely worked, or grew empty as the air, in the thinner handling of its attenuation.

They are not angry for the cause, but angry for they're angry: the condition assuming the cause to legitimise itself.

There is no one who could not be seduced, at some time, by somebody; but the desire for fidelity precludes that coincidence.

A guilty feeling of undeserving that reconstructs relationships in which its feelings are forever unreciprocated.

We forget what we really know.

Everything comes to us, if it come to us at all.

Conflict between desire and self-possession, as between an itch and the resistance to scratch, which only aggravates its condition.

Whereas I left off listening to that music because I wanted to get a distance from its passion and pathos, I begin to seek it again; as the resonance of the very emotion that I now so desire to keep alive.

Strange, that had I ever met Shelley, I would have been as bored by his opinions as he by my diffidence, and silence; who so intimately share, in his 'Triumph of Life', his brilliant-dark vision—the equipoise of loveliness and futility. And whose despair should be our deepest consolation too.

Brouwer's leering vision, of ale-house peasants, pissing in corners, cheating one another at cards, smashing flagons over each other's heads, I find too grotesquely true.

I would have told them, but they never asked me in the way I wanted.

Who identify with masks are nothing in themselves.

An itch which prompts me recognise its cause.

All one can really do for humankind is to pursue one's own emancipation, one's own individuation. For the most one can offer others is one's own example, one's own truth.

Feminine longing, more imaginative, sensuous, and diffuse.

How refreshing, in a world of hypocrisy and dissimilation, to hear in Coriolanus such fine accent of contempt and scorn.

For the person I left her for, I find not a trace of feeling.

At our most unrepressed, are we not at our most mad?

As a butterfly comes to trust where it settles.

It is part of that journey, when I try to write, that I encounter anew, the wraiths of emptiness and worthlessness, which remind me once more of the motive that compels me.

Without the courage to see her reality, she forever hides in denial; whilst her experience grows a continual antagonism to her, representing the reality she refuses to accept.

   Is it inseparable, the drive to create, from a want of identity, and the need to come into being?

What does it matter that we leave, since we can know, or feel, nothing of what we leave behind.

By my first real injury, I discovered my original weakness—and when my life force begins to ebb, and flow back towards itself, I always feel the same dull strain in my lower back—like an objection, and regression, confronted with uncomfortable change.

'As the sapless foliage of the ocean', I am subject to my own continuous ferment and upheaval, with the same sway over myself.

A photograph of the Syrian conflict—a little girl sprawled like a doll in a deserted street, in an attitude of death that seemed more eloquent of the pain of life than any agony; that dimly conscious pain which makes us all victims, and finally desire to suffer no more.

You can tell they're slag by the way they walk.

In reading, and in people, I am (we are) always too idle, shallow, and ingenuous.

To allow to her the same desires undoes, in part, their jealousy; for what we can admit to, we begin to cease to fear.

About whom it was written, or in what mood of disgust or ennui, is no longer important, if it stand beyond the moment.

I was cut with those feelings, in my unguarded youth and ardour.

In memory, it is not I who remember, but I who am remembered: I am the subject of my memory.

A haemorrhage of thoughts.

She makes me feel the way she was made to feel; and I become the voice of her own objection—prevented in the spontaneity that was prevented in her.

Her lack of response made me mistrust my own instincts.

It fascinates me, that Shakespeare should take so little interest to collect his works. Is this carelessness of his posterity, perhaps, our greatest clue to what he understood about human life?

I am more comprehended by teenage girls, than middle aged men, who understand me intellectually by *feeling*.

How much sense in writing is conveyed through the sounding of reading, when it listens to itself;—particularly in the pronunciation of assonance?

Nothing estranges like incomprehension.

Her concern really an extension of her anxiety.

'To those that have shall be given'—for what they have is a freedom from overdetermination, and an ability to listen.

The rage, abjection, and confusion of so many at their end, is more telling about our human condition than any comfort, or consolation.

The difference between biography as an assemblage of research, and narrative of facts, and that plangent identification with the subject, that involvement and response, where facts merely subserve the loving delineation of a portrait (Eisler). As the most objective interpretations of music are the most strongly personal.

A church as witness of history, expression of art and aspiration; and religion as the evolving ritual of an endless human need.

I do not end, nor has the objective world, so called, a reality, and alterity, beyond myself; but I am circumstance and agent, mind and body, wave and particle, continuous and discrete.

Intuition is a discerning and identification of the same motive within oneself. To understand her, I have to find her in myself.

Those who find themselves through the job they do, as their vocation; and those who can imagine themselves as doing many things, who feel a less fundamental want of identity.

It is a testament to her that she took the most insightful and empathetic photographs of me, who, until then, was never recorded in a way that was not uncomfortable or self-conscious.

I no longer belong to that time.

A vacancy, beyond regret or desire.

I subverted opportunity, as a child viciously spoils its own drawing.

Insight only comes when we are strong enough to admit it.

Cassandra-like, the madness of a dream magnifies details, trifles, to telling truths; whose significance disturbs us with the recognition of their *denial*.

One cannot get to the end of pain, except to recover oneself: for pain is the infinity of loss, of oneself in the other; of both loss, and lost.

Looking for return, in order to justify oneself, one's identity, through the *other*; rather than finding that sufficiency in *oneself*.

Pain,—intrinsic to all creation, and coming into being,—as inseparable from phenomenal life, all individuality, and difference; and actually the ground for its expression.

What is belief, but the desire that something be true—so as to justify a preconception, or predisposition, in oneself.

It is the vengeful alone who take revenge,—and her revenge is not upon me but her own abjection.

Constable's oil sketches, visceral and instinctive in their rich impasto, convey the deepest sense of life; as weather, impermanence, and driving change.

Our common enemy is fanaticism.

I have read things praised which to my mind were utterly insipid, and marvelled at that difference of perception, which seemed to me so overdetermined by the desire to praise.

It is characteristic of my latent idealism that when I achieve anything I as quickly despise it, as a hopeless disappointment; before I learn to appreciate it, as I get to know it. From whence also that strain of credulity, which is surprised to be so disappointed.

The terror behind all pretension, which is both its motive, and the self to which it is finally betrayed.

How to reconcile the pain one causes, even in good faith: to take responsibility for it, rather than permit, as in 'Don Juan', those blanks, and silences, which cry out to us for redress.

They can never find it who cannot make an end.

We sense in their behaviour an appearance or reality, as it is conscious or unconscious of its effect.

'That nature must compel us to lament our most persisted deeds'. Consciousness is the synthesis achieved through opposition, frustration, failure, and disappointment; from a lack of adaptation. Out of which there emerges the similar antagonism of will and fate.

The apparent arbitrariness of many dreams and recollections testifies rather to the strangeness and irreverence of association; where things prompt and suggest each other for reasons more flippant, trivial and playful.

Against an infinity of blue, between the giant arches of its ruins, the swifts in their sudden changes arc, with a brief unbidden joy.

Under that intense sun, beneath the Palatine Hill, she struck me like the vision of a dream. Unobserved in her imperceptible motion, amidst the blind and changing currents of the crowd, she was muffled in a strange scarf; her eyes, lost in shadow, bent with her tiny frame towards the earth. With her nerveless hand urging at no one a cup or bowl, the shudder of worthless coins, at haunting intervals, resounded like a knell from another world. Strangely awed, I stooped with her, and whispered: "Signora, …degli spiccioli".

There was something intent and insistent about their pose and smile; their 'selfie': something formulaic, repetitious, and collusive, as it were addressed to the world. Which reminded me of other photographs I had myself taken; but which were rather composed by the moment: spontaneous, unself-conscious, more about ourselves, and for ourselves; not so much smiling as gazing at some shared content.

What is 'personality disorder' (like so many other modern 'diagnoses' which mistake behaviour for illness)—how can a personality be 'disordered'—except when it fails to accord with a prescription of what personality, or more properly behaviour, ought to be. Behaviour, which is the expression of personality (in both its sickness and health,) is simply the communication of what we are. As quality of mind cannot be ordered or disordered, its description, and diagnosis, should be 'foul'; both in its intention and effect.

When I consider the reaction of others (particularly those closest to me) to my poems, I shudder at their incomprehension; and at the pointlessness of my writing when its very purpose is communication. Where I hoped that with a little patience, their difficulties might resolve, and sound and sense like resonance, with each line, grow with reading, I am resigned now to blankness and silence. And I wonder at myself; and my ability to make of my experience something coherent and comprehensible, when I am unable to convey it. Perhaps, the point at last, is that I am now strong enough through writing them to accept their rejection, and my isolation, and be content to remain not understood; which is our human fate.

I would rather begin with the presumption of our *worthlessness*. For the presumption of worth is more often contradicted, in disillusion, and the defeat of expectation, both in ourselves and others.

Though I survive, perhaps, in some trace, echo, or haunting, in eternity, throw my ashes to the wind, as worthless in themselves. If the law confers on us dignity and equality, in human life there is really little dignity, and less equality; little interest, and less value, in our individual selves than we pretend. And it is the exceptional life alone which leaves behind more than their empty profession.

More than snobbery, I have always found that there is nothing more hateful, more resenting, than the envy of the mob: more prevalent and pernicious; that more vehemently denies what it secretly knows, in pretending to political legitimacy.

A history now too full of incident to recall, but which is preserved in my abiding feeling.

A chance, like the fall of dice, appearing random in itself, but whose consequences fall within the stream of necessity—looking before and after—and which cannot be separated from its circumstance.

Who in feeling find and recognise themselves.

Blame is finally irrelevant: for what matters, what remains, is our feelings, and their relation to ourselves.

At a Goya exhibition. Trying to understand the quality of presence in his finest portraits, I was led to consider those of his declining years: the anonymous phantoms—figments of the moment—blinking in and out of existence; as if the illumination which beheld and felt now perceived only unsubstantial air.

When we are thoughtless, we are most suggestible to the thought of others, thinking of us.

Despite our best meaning, we are the terrible occasion of pain we can neither control nor alleviate. For we must play our part not for ourselves alone.

The power of Shakespeare, like the moon, to draw what's dim in us and undiscovered from the darkness of our own sea.

Across the bay, the headland's sight, looming from the mist of distance, the weather brightening along it, was like an imagination of enduring life.

The resenters—those praters of morality; without the courage to do what they presume to judge, searching for the mistakes they are afraid to make; they live as parasites on the actions of others for their ideology of revenge.

If humankind is to survive, we must evolve a far keener sense of our capacity for self-deception. We are invariably deceived through an ignorance of ourselves; but what is dangerous is that willing ignorance, our self-righteousness, which projects upon others what is unacceptable to itself. This is most acute, and inveterate, in faith and religion, where hatred and vilification is most highly defended.

Our surreptitious wills we betray to ourselves. As Capulet, in urging the marriage feast; who finds himself below stairs in his own kitchen, to hurry on those ambitions for Juliet, which she now threatens to frustrate, and which, for the first time, he acknowledges as his own. So our selfish desires grow most insistent at the very point of their overthrow.

On some portraits by Moroni. In their pride and reserve, they defer only to propriety; their reticence an evasive hauteur, or humility: and the common and familiar, a provocation to what we cannot know—to what they cannot, or they will not, share.

Suicide is less an act, of will, or of revenge, but a ghostly motion, which usurps reason and decision; an infinite sense of nothing, and desire for the sea.

More joyful, and intimate, despite its short duration, and despite its deceptions, more honest, and courageous; because we met our pain.

When we see in others what we remain blind to in ourselves, we are holding off a truth we cannot accept; as we refuse to connect our physical illness with emotional sickness.

We re-experience the pain until there comes, or does not come, the insight into why it is we continue to feel it: that it is, not to ourselves, but of ourselves—that in that pain, we stand in eternal relation to a primal experience. As I once felt myself to be, abandoned, worthless, and bereft—and ever after looking on at an intimacy and richness I could only envy.

An ordinary and instinctive response to what is physically attractive, but which forms no part of that dialectic with myself. A dialectic which now gives to my experience an austere clarity; that unless it reappear, it must necessarily lack real significance.

The control and severity in that music is a pathos of my own, and I hear it because I have found it in myself.

The opt-out, stay-at-home fathers, who obsequiously smile at those mothers also pushing prams; hoping that through them, they might legitimise their abrogation as men.

Those who refer psychological phenomena to physical changes, chemistry, etc., propose causes inadequate for what they seek to explain. To reduce complex things in order to explain 'how' they occur, they exclude precisely what is necessary to understand them, the larger question of 'why'. The 'why' of happening is not reducible, for it lies in things greater and more complex still.

I wonder if the pain of dying, irrespective of its expression, is not just the unassimilated agony of life.

Even in those first exchanges, there was writ in small the text of all our subsequent conflict.

What is politics but a dressed-up personal resentment; or self-justification through what one professes to believe. And what we profess and protest to the world, what is it more than a desire to legitimise ambition, and the applause it seeks.

An ethereal sadness, like the damp of a laurel grove which the sun never penetrates. Edward Thomas.

With her determined singing to prevent the child from crying, she conveyed, and so provoked, the very anxiety that she sought to forestall; her fear of crying.

The feel of someone's eyes; the projection from them of a thought; which makes one conscious of them.

There is a time to stop, when we become weary to ourselves... How few of those books which I once enjoyed, with such openness and receptivity, can I now bear to reread. As we turn from what we are not, as we achieve ourselves, we tire of what we are: and I would not become tedious (if I had one) to my reader.

We should learn to as lightly leave as we are left.

To treat circumstance as accidental to character; that had such and such happened, or not happened, the destiny of an individual would have been otherwise; is to embark on a speculation necessarily infinite. To treat a character, such as Hamlet, in the abstract, is to divest him of the very circumstances which make him actual. A Hamlet not born into these circumstances is another entity, call him what you will.

For to be realised as such, as Hamlet, these contingencies, so called, become the necessary conditions for the very character we know: 'To punish me with this and this with me'—the means by which he confronts himself. We exist as individuals—as phenomena—in the concrete; not abstracted from a world from which we are inseparable.

Dear Sir/Madam,

I am writing in recollection of a conversation, some thirty years ago, before a walk in high summer to Stevington Mill. Friends who farmed in Bletsoe had spoken of the ghost of a Spitfire, or other fighter plane from the Second World War, which appeared along the railway cutting en route to the mill. Whether Spitfires ever flew over Stevington, I don't know, but I was raised in north Bedfordshire, between the old airfields of Little Staughton and Thurleigh, and the imagination of those days still fills those empty skies. The short piece I include is my last, and a curious testament to the duration of memory.

Yours faithfully,
N. S. A. Parsons

In her incredulous grief, and the appeal of her pain, she disturbed me with a measureless distress: a feeling *for* her which had discovered that sorrow in myself.

What moves me, in the great medieval music of the church, is the faith that I *cannot* share—as it rises, in the lonely majesty of its setting, the terrible poignance of those voices roused in hope and despair.

Someone said that we do not find, but we create, ourselves. But is not creation a potentiation; and could we create what is not latent in ourselves. Is life not the potentiation that *is* creation, and the finding of ourselves?

The conceit, that through medical intervention, we might indefinitely live on. That blindness, to the arc of our own life; to its decline; to our own conclusion. Unwilling to give way to what must succeed ourselves; to accept our insignificance in nature; to allow a fitness in the time to die. To will life, for the *sake* of living on; are we not willing, with our increasing irrelevance, only the prolongation of our own decay. For human life should learn to *justify* itself, and not merely *to* itself.

There is no 'royal road' in my dreams, but they remain opaque, as if they kept a business of their own.

An eternal moment beneath the evergreen oaks; in the sunlight and first suggestion of autumn: as one stood in relation to one's whole life.

One either stages that drama within the context of one's life, or it is staged in the circumstances of one's death.

A madness of pain: the impetus to becoming; which life provokes and antagonises into the actuality which is its objectivity, and self-consciousness; and the bitter truth of our reality.

To disentangle oneself from what does not matter: what does *not* concern oneself; the people one cares *nothing for*; what one *cannot change*.

Each parturition a new expression of the conflict, which is a working out of an ongoing family heredity.

Stubbs 'Haymakers' and 'Reapers' compose a vision of the sacrifice and submission required of humankind to civilisation. The conscious contrivance of form and attitude, the strain of discipline *self*-imposed—in the haymakers—and *im*posed—in the reapers—to create order, both in the human and the natural world.

Given what we are in relation to everything else, the only end possible to ourselves. 'Where there is no transcendent purpose, there can be no contingency'.

Coincidence, correlation, connection, causation. Where we purport to demonstrate agency—as we read constantly with regard to illness—that such and such a thing is the 'cause' of such and such another—we have increasingly to demonstrate knowledge itself.

Who in their service move with that aloofness which is superior to those they serve.

Where before it was God who seemed remote, it now appears that it is we who are too close to ourselves to *see* purpose.

Where life is a long climb to surmount the suffering of our dependency and credulity, one cannot look behind one but with contempt: for what is *beneath* oneself; for what one *has* been; and for those who, at any age, remind us of it.

We live as if life owed something to us, when it is we who are owing to nature—who lends out of herself—a debt to be recalled.

From the struggle between inward and outward pressure, through the '*imaginative elaboration* of physical parts, feelings and functions', there evolves the psyche. Out of the psyche, there arises the mind; from those experiences we *cannot* assimilate, as the means to make sense of them. For the mind *conceives* itself through *opposition*. From this abstraction derives the sense of a self independent of its physiology; and a defensive assumption of what we *are*, and *ought* to be. So, what we cannot reconcile, we ascribe to causes accidental to us—like injury, illness and disease—and what we do not wish to accept, as happening by chance: concepts that do not exist *but* for the mind. Preserving ourselves from the pain and responsibility of our fatality.

An upwelling, in which appear, rise and subside, strange narratives; of questions and contradictions; agitation and contention; fascination and fear: whose richness we exclude, and deny, to preserve the idea, and ideal, of ourselves.

That feeling, recollecting 'Tess'; as the staring, in mute agony, of some ghastly wound; where death is merely waiting to die.

The clouds in peaks arise like distant longing.

Sketch for a proposed last poem, of value to the author as a recognition of the end of his desire. The *desire* to compose—to sustain the tension, for thought and feeling to coalesce… A want of purpose, due, in part, to an increasing bleakness of vision, which he no longer wishes to pursue. He understands with this attempt he has left his writing behind.

As road-carrion stirred by the wind alone
Of its unseperable soul bereft
the bubble breaks of time
as deft
life closes with the sphere
in its eclipse, as empty left
as objectless eyes
Of all affection and regret, desire and fear

The dignity of animals, without words creed cant tears Resign with quiet what they called their own To live in nature with the humility to know there is no more Our truth lies in the shadow of faith—in what we do not want to believe know

The lithe hare quaveringly alive
whose fears at last their end contrive
The kite, in its keen drift abstract and clear
should cryless disappear
And bee
commended to its brevity
waving in the flowers
to dally with the lightsome hours
to press into the flower to die